THE FANTASTICALLY FUNNY KNOCK KNOCK JOKE BOOK

ARCTURUS

ARCTURUS

This edition published in 2016 by Arcturus Publishing Limited
26/27 Bickels Yard, 151–153 Bermondsey Street,
London SE1 3HA

ISBN: 978-1-78599-306-0
CH004985NT
Supplier 29, Date 0516, Print run 5104

Written by Lisa Regan
Designed by Trudi Webb
Edited by Rebecca Clunes
Illustrations from Shutterstock

Printed in China

CONTENTS

1 JOKES TO TELL YOUR FRIENDS 5

2 JOKES THAT'LL SPLIT YOUR SIDES..........37

3 JOKES THAT'LL CHEER YOU UP..................69

4 JOKES TO TELL YOUR FAMILY.................... 101

5 JOKES THAT'LL MAKE YOU GROAN 132

6 JOKES TO TELL YOUR TEACHER............. 165

7 JOKES THAT'LL HAVE YOU IN STITCHES 197

8 JOKES TO TELL YOUR DOG 229

KNOCK, KNOCK.
WHO'S THERE?
BOO!
BOO WHO?
DON'T CRY, I'M ONLY JOKING!

KNOCK, KNOCK.
WHO'S THERE?
ALLY.
ALLY WHO?
ALLYGATORS AREN'T THE SAME AS CROCODILES, YOU KNOW!

KNOCK, KNOCK.
WHO'S THERE?
SONIA.
SONIA WHO?
SONIA DRESS, YOU MUST HAVE SAT IN IT AT THE PARK.

KNOCK, KNOCK.
WHO'S THERE?
CARMEN.
CARMEN WHO?
CARMEN PLAY BALL OUTSIDE!

KNOCK, KNOCK.
WHO'S THERE?
DONNA.
DONNA WHO?
DONNA YOU WANNA COME FOR PIZZA WITH US?

KNOCK, KNOCK.
WHO'S THERE?
CHRIS.
CHRIS WHO?
CHRIS-PY BACON FOR BREAKFAST, MMMM!

15

31

KNOCK, KNOCK.
WHO'S THERE?
ANNIE.
ANNIE WHO?
ANNIE THING WRONG?
YOU HAVEN'T BEEN OUT
LATELY.

KNOCK, KNOCK.
WHO'S THERE?
JOE KING.
JOE KING WHO?
JOKING, AREN'T
YOU? IT'S ME!

KNOCK, KNOCK.
WHO'S THERE?
EVAN.
EVAN WHO?
EVAN THOUGH IT'S LATE,
WON'T YOU
LET ME IN?

39

KNOCK, KNOCK.
WHO'S THERE?
ANITA.
ANITA WHO?
ANITA USE YOUR PHONE, PLEASE!

KNOCK, KNOCK.
WHO'S THERE?
BELLA.
BELLA WHO?
BELLA THE BALL IN MY NEW DRESS!

KNOCK, KNOCK.
WHO'S THERE?
DWAYNE.
DWAYNE WHO?
DWAYNES ARE BLOCKED AND SMELL REALLY BAD!

47

53

57

59

KNOCK, KNOCK.
WHO'S THERE?
OLIVIA.
OLIVIA WHO?
OLIVIA, STUPID, BUT YOU'VE LOCKED ME OUT.

KNOCK, KNOCK.
WHO'S THERE?
POLICE.
POLICE WHO?
POLICE CAN I COME IN AND USE YOUR PHONE!

KNOCK, KNOCK.
WHO'S THERE?
HANNAH.
HANNAH WHO?
HANNAH 1, 2, 3, 4, EVERYBODY JOIN IN!

KNOCK, KNOCK.
WHO'S THERE?
SIDNEY.
SIDNEY WHO?
SID NEEDS YOUR HELP
TO FIX HIS CAR.

KNOCK, KNOCK.
WHO'S THERE?
TRISTAN.
TRISTAN WHO?
TRISTAN-ICE GIRL
LIKE YOU TO HELP
YOUR LITTLE
SISTER.

KNOCK, KNOCK.
WHO'S THERE?
ALBERT.
ALBERT WHO?
ALBERT YOU CAN'T GUESS
WHO IT IS?!

85

91

93

KNOCK, KNOCK.
WHO'S THERE?
CONNOR.
CONNOR WHO?
CONNOR CHEETAH RUN
FASTER THAN A CAR?

KNOCK, KNOCK.
WHO'S THERE?
ARMY.
ARMY WHO?
ARMY FRIENDS
ALLOWED HERE
TO PLAY?

KNOCK, KNOCK.
WHO'S THERE?
BABY.
BABY WHO?
BABY I'LL GED RID OB
DIS CODE SOON.

105

115

KNOCK, KNOCK.
WHO'S THERE?
IDA.
IDA WHO?
IDA KNOW WHY NO ONE WILL PLAY OUTSIDE!

KNOCK, KNOCK.
WHO'S THERE?
BART.
BART WHO?
BART TIME YOU GOT UP, IT'S 12 O'CLOCK!

KNOCK, KNOCK.
WHO'S THERE?
POLICE.
POLICE WHO?
POLICE FIX YOUR DOORBELL, MY KNUCKLES ARE GETTING SORE!

121

125

KNOCK, KNOCK.
WHO'S THERE?
BARBARA.
BARBARA WHO?
BARBARA FOR NOW,
SEE YOU LATER!

KNOCK, KNOCK.
WHO'S THERE?
ANNA.
ANNA WHO?
ANNA-NOTHER ONE
BITES THE DUST.

KNOCK, KNOCK.
WHO'S THERE?
BRIANNA.
BRIANNA WHO?
BRIANNA CRANBERRY
BAGUETTE–DO YOU WANT A
BITE?

135

140

141

146

147

149

KNOCK, KNOCK.
WHO'S THERE?
GUS.
GUS WHO?
GUS OF WIND BLEW DOWN THE BIRD FEEDER!

KNOCK, KNOCK.
WHO'S THERE?
EWAN.
EWAN WHO?
EWAN ME SHOULD GO OUT SOMETIME.

KNOCK, KNOCK.
WHO'S THERE?
OMAN.
OMAN WHO?
OMAN, I LEFT MY HOMEWORK ON MY BED!

157

159

163

KNOCK, KNOCK.
WHO'S THERE?
PIZZA!
PIZZA WHO?
PIZZA THE ACTION!

KNOCK, KNOCK.
WHO'S THERE?
CELESTE.
CELESTE WHO?
CELESTE TIME I'M COMING OVER TO HELP WITH YOUR HOMEWORK.

KNOCK, KNOCK.
WHO'S THERE?
CATH.
CATH WHO?
I KNEW YOU WERE NUTS!

KNOCK, KNOCK.
WHO'S THERE?
THOMAS.
THOMAS WHO?
THOMAS JUST GOT A NEW KITTEN. COME AND SEE IT!

KNOCK, KNOCK.
WHO'S THERE?
BEN HUR.
BEN HUR WHO?
BEN HUR AN HOUR. DIDN'T YOU HEAR ME KNOCKING?

KNOCK, KNOCK.
WHO'S THERE?
JIM.
JIM WHO?
JIM MIND IF I HAVE A BITE?

KNOCK, KNOCK.
WHO'S THERE?
SEAN.
SEAN WHO?
SEAN YOUR HAIR
AGAIN, HAVE YOU?

KNOCK, KNOCK.
WHO'S THERE?
AMAL.
AMAL WHO?
AMAL SHOOK UP,
UH HUH HUH.

KNOCK, KNOCK.
WHO'S THERE?
MCKEE.
MCKEE WHO?
MCKEE WON'T TURN IN
THE LOCK!

189

KNOCK, KNOCK.
WHO'S THERE?
HARRY.
HARRY WHO?
HARRY UP, WE'LL BE LATE FOR GYM!

KNOCK, KNOCK.
WHO'S THERE?
SCOTT.
SCOTT WHO?
SCOTT TO BE SAID, YOUR BEDROOM IS A MESS!

KNOCK, KNOCK.
WHO'S THERE?
KEN.
KEN WHO?
KEN YOU MOVE YOUR BIKE, IT'S BLOCKING THE PATH!

217

227

CHAPTER 8

JOKES TO TELL YOUR DOG

KNOCK, KNOCK.
WHO'S THERE?
DUMMY.
DUMMY WHO?
DUMMY A SANDWICH, WILL YOU? I'M HUNGRY!

KNOCK, KNOCK.
WHO'S THERE?
JUAN.
JUAN WHO?
JUAN TO HEAR MORE JOKES?

KNOCK, KNOCK.
WHO'S THERE?
DOZEN.
DOZEN WHO?
DOZEN ANYONE EVER READ THE NEWSPAPERS?

KNOCK, KNOCK.
WHO'S THERE?
COLIN.
COLIN WHO?
COLIN YOU TO HELP ME WITH ALGEBRA HOMEWORK!

KNOCK, KNOCK.
WHO'S THERE?
PAULA.
PAULA WHO?
PAULA DOOR OPEN, AND LET THE SUN SHINE IN!

KNOCK, KNOCK.
WHO'S THERE?
MAJOR.
MAJOR WHO?
MAJOR JUMP, HA HA!

239

243

253